Cornerstones of Freedom

The Story of
SUSAN B. ANTHONY

By Susan Clinton

Illustrated by Ralph Canaday

CHILDRENS PRESS ®

CHICAGO

Library of Congress Cataloging-in-Publication Data

Clinton, Susan.
   The story of Susan B. Anthony.

   (Cornerstones of freedom)
   Summary: Recounts the story of the nineteenth-century
activist who spent much of her life fighting for women's
rights.
   1. Anthony, Susan B. (Susan Brownell), 1820-1906—
Juvenile literature.   2. Suffragettes—United States—
Biography—Juvenile literature.   3. Feminists—United
States—Biography—Juvenile literature.   4. Women's
rights—United States—Juvenile literature.
[1. Anthony, Susan B. (Susan Brownell), 1820-1906.
   2. Feminists. 3. Women's rights]   I. Canaday, Ralph,
ill.   II. Title.   III. Series.
HQ1413.A55C55   1986   324.6′23′0924 [B] [92]   86-9613
ISBN 0-516-04705-1

At 7 A.M. on November 5, 1872, Susan B. Anthony broke the law by doing something she had never done before. After twenty years of working to win the vote for women, she marched to the polls in Rochester, New York, and voted. Her vote—for Ulysses S. Grant for president—was illegal. In New York State, only men were allowed to vote. Women could vote in only two states—Wyoming and Utah.

The penalties for breaking the law were stiff—up to three years in prison and a fine of as much as $500. But Susan B. Anthony believed she had found a way around state law. She claimed to be relying on a higher law—the Fourteenth Amendment to the United States Constitution. Her argument was good enough to convince the election judges. But the real test began two weeks later when she was arrested for voting illegally.

Even while being arrested, Anthony insisted on equal treatment. The marshal was embarrassed to arrest this gray-haired, dignified, fifty-two-year-old woman. But she forced him to bring her in, instead of letting her report on her own. She loudly insisted that the marshal pay her streetcar fare. She even tried to make the marshal handcuff her, but he refused. Against her wishes, her lawyer, Henry R. Selden, paid her bail.

Once out on bail, Anthony wanted the public to know what she had done and why. She spent the next seven months explaining her case in Ohio, Indiana, Illinois, and, above all, New York State, where her trial would be held. She gave copies of her arguments to congressmen and newspaper editors. Whether the New York newspapers poked fun at her or praised her, they gave Anthony the publicity she needed. Her own speeches won her admirers. One woman who heard her speak at a women's convention said, "No, I am not converted to what these women advocate. I am too cowardly for that; but I am converted to Susan B. Anthony."

Anthony's argument rested on the wording of the Fourteenth Amendment. The congressmen who wrote that amendment certainly did not intend to give women the vote. Instead, the amendment was meant to give the vote to all black former slaves in the South. It forbids any state to pass a law that keeps any citizen from voting. According to the amendment, "citizens" are "all persons born or naturalized in the United States." Well, Anthony reasoned, wasn't she a person born in the United States, and, therefore, a citizen? Then how could any state law keep her from voting?

She was not the first to think of this argument. Many lawyers and lawmakers could see that the wording of the amendment was unclear. In her speeches she said, "We ask the judges to render true and unprejudiced opinions of the law, and wherever there is room for doubt to give its benefit on the side of liberty and equal rights to women."

At her trial, on June 17, 1873, Anthony was not allowed to speak in her own defense. She listened while Selden argued her case. After hearing both sides, Judge Ward Hunt pronounced her guilty. Later he fined her $100. Angry and disappointed, Anthony declared, "I shall never pay a dollar of your unjust penalty."

Anthony never did pay the fine. Nor did she let this setback stop her. She was to spend the rest of her life, the next thirty-three years, fighting for women's rights. She had the courage to take risks for her beliefs. She also had what is perhaps greater courage—to work steadily for them, year after year. Finally, in 1920, the Nineteenth Amendment granted the vote to women. Anthony did not live to see it—she died in 1906. But it is often called the Susan B. Anthony Amendment in her honor.

When Anthony began working for women's rights, many people came to hear her because they had never heard a woman speaker before. Although women could address women's meetings, it was shocking for a woman to lecture to a mixed audience.

Later in Anthony's career, people came to get a look at the sour, mannish spinster they had seen in newspaper cartoons. What they saw instead was a slender, ladylike woman wearing a lace-collared dress and a bonnet. Anthony had a wide mouth that turned down at the corners. Newspapers turned this into a forbidding frown and dismissed her as a frustrated old maid. But people who heard her in person were usually surprised by her warmth, sincerity, and humor.

Anthony's cause was unpopular and she suffered a great deal of ridicule and abuse for it. Women, as well as men, believed that "delicate womenfolk" belonged in the home, not in public life. However, running a home in the nineteenth century was hardly delicate work. On laundry day, for example, most women had to pump water for the laundry tubs and stir the clothes into boiling water. Women cooked on wood- or coal-burning stoves, pressed clothes with irons weighing up to ten pounds, and made most of the family's clothes by hand. Caring for children had to fit in between a housewife's other tasks.

Born in 1820, Susan Brownell Anthony was the second of eight children. As they grew up in western New York, the Anthony girls learned to help their worn and silent mother, Lucy Read Anthony, with the housework. Susan's father, Daniel Anthony, ran a textile mill. Most of the factory workers were young girls who tended weaving machines from 6 A.M. to 6 P.M. every day except Sundays.

Factory work was one of the few jobs open to unmarried women. Wages were low by today's standards. When Susan filled in for a girl who was sick, she earned $1.50 a week. Most of the employees were also boarders—they lived in the Anthonys' home. The factory workers probably enjoyed having money of their own and being free of housework. Susan's mother, on the other hand, had to care for her family and cook for all the boarders too.

Taking in boarders was one way for a married woman to make extra money. Married women could also take in laundry or do extra sewing, but the money they earned did not belong to them. Whatever a wife earned or inherited belonged, by law, to her husband. When Daniel Anthony's factory failed in 1838, all of his wife's possessions, even her clothes, were sold to help pay his debts.

Perhaps the example of her mother's life helped convince Susan B. Anthony not to marry, even though she had offers. Later on, her work was so important to her that she did not want to give it up for marriage. As she saw fellow reformers drop out of the movement in order to marry and have children, she wrote in discouragement: "There is not one woman left who may be relied on. All have first to please their husbands after which there is little time or energy left to spend in any other direction."

If Anthony's early life helped her see the problems in women's lives, she also gained the courage and confidence to do something about them. Susan's father was a Quaker. He raised his children in the Quaker belief that women were equal to men. Susan's father was also proud of her intelligence. For a while, he sent her to a girls' boarding school in Philadelphia. This, too, was unusual.

Most parents didn't think that girls needed much education. At the time, only one college in the country, Oberlin in Ohio, accepted women. The only career open to women was teaching. So that was the job Susan took up to help pay her father's debts. She found that she could earn from $2.00 to $2.50 a week, one-fourth the salary a male teacher earned.

One of the first places where Susan B. Anthony spoke out for women's rights was at a teachers' convention in 1853. All three hundred female teachers sat in the back listening to the men discuss "Why the profession of teacher is not as much respected as that of lawyer, doctor, or minister." Everyone was surprised when Anthony asked to speak. After debating, the men decided to hear her out. She startled them by saying, "Do you not see that so long as society says woman has not brains enough to be a doctor, lawyer, or minister, but has plenty to be a teacher, every man of you who condescends to teach tacitly admits . . . that he has no more brains than a woman?"

After fifteen years of teaching, Anthony had saved $300. She returned to Rochester, New York, to find her family deeply involved in the most important reform movements of the times—antislavery, women's rights, and temperance. Her father was doing well in the insurance business now. He was ready to support her in whatever work she chose. She started cautiously with the most conventional reform movement, temperance.

Temperance reformers wanted people to stop drinking alcoholic beverages. At the time, alcohol

was easy to buy in general stores, saloons were common, and many men drank heavily. Drinking husbands were a serious problem for wives who could not protect themselves or their children from debt or abuse. Respectable women had been forming temperance groups, and Anthony joined one such group, the Rochester Daughters of Temperance.

Her experiences in temperance work gradually brought Anthony into the fight for women's rights. For one thing, she found she was a good organizer. She was soon elected president of her temperance group. Then, on the way home from a temperance convention, she met the bold and eloquent Elizabeth Cady Stanton, one of the moving forces behind the new women's rights movement.

Stanton had helped organize the first women's rights convention in 1848. She wrote out the goals of the convention in her Declaration of Sentiments. The most controversial one called for women to win suffrage, or the right to vote. Anthony's parents went to the convention. Impressed and converted, they both signed the Declaration of Sentiments.

Ever since her family told her about the convention, Anthony had wanted to meet Elizabeth Cady Stanton. When the two women finally met, they struck up an immediate friendship. Stanton encouraged Anthony to attend her first women's rights convention in 1852. Here Anthony heard many impressive women speakers.

She agreed with them on several issues. The problems Anthony met in her temperance work convinced her that women were virtually powerless.

Her women's groups broke up because none of the
women had any money of their own. And without the
vote, women had little power to change laws. On top
of that, Anthony was not even allowed to speak at
the men's state temperance convention. The chair-
man said, "The sisters were not invited here to
speak, but to listen and learn."

Angry at this, Anthony and a small group of followers walked out. They decided to form their own Woman's State Temperance Society. Stanton was elected president and Anthony secretary of the new society.

Both men and women were allowed to join their society. But at the second convention, in 1853, men began to take over.

Anthony resigned in frustration. That was the end of her temperance work and the beginning of her work for women's rights.

Together Susan B. Anthony and Elizabeth Cady Stanton led the women's rights movement for over fifty years. Anthony had the freedom to travel, organizing speaking tours and conventions. Stanton, married with seven children, spoke in person when she could and sent speeches when she couldn't. Stanton later described their teamwork: "In thought and sympathy we were one, and in the division of labor we exactly complemented each other. I am the better writer, she the better critic. She supplied facts and statistics, I the philosophy and rhetoric, and, together, we have made arguments that have stood unshaken through the storms of long years; arguments that no one has answered."

Their first goal was property rights for married women. Stanton wrote a petition. It asked that married women be able to keep any money they earned themselves. Anthony called a convention. There she recruited sixty women, one to cover each county in New York State. Anthony herself covered the Rochester area, trudging from door to door asking people to sign her petition. The signatures were needed to show that people wanted this reform. Getting them wasn't easy.

The only way to travel from town to town was by stagecoach or sled. In the winter, the trips were cold and bumpy. Some hotels wouldn't take a lone woman for fear she was not respectable. As she tramped through the cold, Anthony found the hardest people to persuade were not men, but women. It was mostly women who slammed doors in her face, saying they didn't need any more rights!

After ten weeks, the women had nearly six thousand signatures—enough to earn a hearing in the

New York legislature. There Stanton delivered a powerful speech. In spite of all their work, the petition was voted down. Anthony and Stanton started over. Stanton wrote pamphlets; Anthony spent yet another winter speaking and collecting signatures all over the state. It was one of New York's coldest winters. Some mornings her hotel room was so cold that she had to break the ice in her pitcher to wash. This time the legislature put off the petition with a joking answer.

Anthony and Stanton started over again. Finally, in 1860, after six years, the legislature was ready to listen. Stanton once again made a speech. The next day the bill passed easily. Women in New York State could now keep their wages. It was an important step toward independence and equality. Speech by speech, name by name, Anthony and Stanton had changed public opinion.

All through the 1850s, the issue of slavery was more and more on people's minds. Some Northern businessmen didn't want to end slavery any more than the Southerners did—their factories needed the cotton that Southern slaves produced. Politicians did not want to face the problem. Only a group of reformers called abolitionists were brave enough

to call for an end to slavery. "No Union with Slaveholders" was their slogan. They wanted the North to break away from the slaveholding South. This idea made people upset and angry; many came to antislavery meetings to heckle and jeer.

Anthony already knew and admired the abolitionists. Her whole family was against slavery. Her father had welcomed leaders such as William Lloyd Garrison, Wendell Phillips, Frederick Douglass, and Parker Pillsbury to his home in Rochester. These reformers also supported Susan B. Anthony's work for women.

In 1856, the abolitionists offered Anthony $10 a week to organize their antislavery campaign in New York State. She accepted. Up through the outbreak of the Civil War, Anthony mustered speakers, arranged meetings, and tried to cope with jeering mobs. In 1860, angry crowds took over halls and shouted down speakers in city after city. In Syracuse, a large dummy labeled "Susan B. Anthony" was dragged through the streets and burned. But Anthony was not to be scared off; she finished the tour.

The Civil War pushed the women's rights campaign into the background. During the war, Anthony and Stanton formed the Women's National Loyal League to launch a petition demanding full freedom for all the slaves. The league collected 400,000 signatures. Every person who signed paid one penny. These pennies were used to pay the league's bills. At the end of the war, the league owed $4.72; Anthony paid this out of her own pocket. Their efforts were rewarded in the Thirteenth Amendment, which freed all the slaves.

Although the slaves were free, they did not have the vote. Anthony thought that abolitionists and women's rights workers should work together in one group. It would work for universal suffrage—voting rights for whites and blacks, men and women. For Anthony and Stanton, the two causes went hand in hand. Both were based on respect for human dignity.

Much to their surprise, the abolitionists refused to help them revive the women's suffrage campaign. They said it was "the Negro's hour." Women would have to wait their turn. Anthony and Stanton were not willing to wait. Anthony said, "I would sooner cut off my right hand than ask for the ballot for the black man and not for woman."

In 1867, the issues of black suffrage and woman suffrage came to a vote in Kansas. But politicians and newspaper editors who had helped women's rights before abandoned the cause now. Anthony and Stanton were back where they had started twenty years earlier, with a group of loyal women, no money, and no political power. As they had twenty years ago, they launched a speaking tour through the whole state. Anthony sold enough of Stanton's pamphlets to pay their bills. They traveled on muddy roads in wagons pulled by mules. Hotel food was greasy, the rooms dirty. Many mornings the two women had to pick bedbugs out of the ruffles on their clothes.

When a wealthy man named George Francis Train offered to help them, Anthony and Stanton were glad to accept.

Audiences loved Train. He openly made fun of reformers such as Garrison and Phillips who refused to help women's rights now. But on election day, both black suffrage and woman suffrage lost. Anthony and Stanton didn't have the money to go home. Train said he would pay for a lecture tour to the East. He also gave them the money to start their own newspaper, the *Revolution*.

The first edition of the *Revolution* came out on January 8, 1868. Stanton and Parker Pillsbury, an antislavery writer, were the editors. Anthony was the publisher. The paper printed news about women's advances and urged reforms such as higher education for women and equal pay for equal work. Some of the topics Stanton wrote about seemed too extreme to many women. Stanton favored easier divorce laws. She wrote about prostitution. She attacked churches for teaching that women were inferior to men.

In addition, many leaders in the women's movement did not like Train. Train had radical ideas about money and banking, and he wrote about them in the *Revolution*. William Lloyd Garrison wrote, "That crack-brained harlequin and semi-lunatic. . . . He is as destitute of principle as he is of sense."

The women's rights leaders also did not agree on what came first, black suffrage or woman suffrage. Lucy Stone and the Bostonians put black suffrage first. Anthony and Stanton led a group that put women first. They argued that if black men got the vote before women, they would join other male voters against woman suffrage. On the other hand, most women would probably vote for black suffrage.

In May 1869, the women's movement split into two groups. Anthony and Stanton took their followers and formed the National Woman Suffrage Association. Lucy Stone answered by forming the American Woman Suffrage Association. As long as the two groups stayed separate, they would compete for women's loyalty. Neither group wanted to divide its following this way, but it took twenty years to reunite them.

One of the events that helped reunite the two groups was the first International Council of Women in 1888. Organizing the event took Anthony and her coworkers a year. The conference was a great success; women from forty-nine countries filled the hall for all eight days. Lucy Stone and other leaders in Stone's American Association accepted Anthony's invitation to speak. By then, the Fourteenth and Fifteenth Amendments had given blacks the vote, but women still did not have it.

In 1870, Anthony gave up on her newspaper. It was $10,000 in debt. To pay it off, she became a professional lecturer. The schedule was demanding. Anthony traveled thousands and thousands of miles speaking about women's rights all over the country. In 1871, she covered eight thousand miles to deliver

108 lectures in Wyoming, Utah, and the Pacific Coast states. At about $100 a week, it took Anthony six years to pay off the *Revolution* debt.

She continued to travel to any state where there was a vote on woman suffrage. In Colorado she rode horseback up mountain trails to reach little mining towns. In South Dakota she rode wagons across the hot, dusty prairie. She went through Kansas in 1894, California in 1895 and 1896, Oregon in 1905.

The companies that made liquor were afraid that women voters would vote them out of business. So liquor makers spent a lot of money to defeat woman suffrage. In Oregon, for example, they required every saloon keeper to recruit twenty-five men to vote against woman suffrage.

Woman suffrage didn't have enough money to defeat the liquor makers. Suffrage lost in state after state. It soon became clear that the best way to win suffrage would be with a constitutional amendment.

In 1878, Anthony convinced Senator Aaron Sargent of California to propose a woman suffrage amendment in the U.S. Senate. The amendment was defeated, but Anthony managed to have it proposed again year after year. She herself spent much time in Washington keeping after politicians and trying to convert them to her cause. In 1904, Anthony spoke to a Senate committee on her amendment for the last time. She said, "We have waited. We stood aside for the Negro; we waited for the millions of immigrants. . . . For all these ignorant, alien peoples, educated women have been compelled to stand aside and wait! How long will this injustice, this outrage continue?"

By now, Anthony was known and respected nationwide. In Oregon she commented, "This is rather different from the receptions I used to get fifty years ago. They threw things at me then—but they were not roses. . . . Now I get flowers instead of eggs." So that their struggle would not be forgotten, Anthony and Stanton gathered all their notebooks, clippings, and letters to write the history of the women's rights movement. Five years later, in 1886, they had succeeded in publishing three fat volumes of the *History of Woman Suffrage;* a fourth volume came out in 1902.

With the help of a journalist friend, Ida Husted Harper, Anthony also put together her own biography. *The Life and Work of Susan B. Anthony, A Story of the Evolution of the Status of Women* was published in 1898.

In 1899, Anthony won a new ally for woman suffrage. One of the most powerful labor unions, the American Federation of Labor, voted to support woman suffrage. Thirty-one years before, the National Labor Union was one of the only labor organizations to accept women. But they did not want anything to do with woman suffrage. Now, working men were beginning to agree with Anthony when she said, "Your own interest demands that you should seek to make women your political equals, for then, instead of being, as now . . . a hindrance to [working men's] efforts to secure better wages and more favorable legislation, the working women would be an added strength, politically, industrially, morally."

The yearly conventions of her National Suffrage
Association had always been very important to
Anthony. In her whole life she missed only two. She
used the conventions to start new campaigns and
bring up new ideas.

Anthony also drew encouragement from these
meetings. She could see that many bright, able
young women were working in the association. In
1900, she felt she could turn its leadership over to
them. She retired from the presidency the day
before her eightieth birthday.

In 1902, Anthony wrote to Stanton, "It is fifty-
one years since we first met and we have been busy
through every one of them, stirring up the world to
recognize the rights of women. . . . We little
dreamed when we began this contest . . . that half a

century later we would be compelled to leave the finish of the battle to another generation of women. But our hearts are filled with joy to know that they enter upon this task equipped with a college education, with business experience, with the freely admitted right to speak in public—all of which were denied to women fifty years ago."

The newspapers called Anthony "the Napoleon of the Women's Rights Movement." She had not succeeded in changing voting laws. By 1906, the year of her death, only four states—Wyoming, Utah, Colorado, and Idaho—gave women the vote. But she had gained wide respect and acceptance for women's rights. Anthony spoke to her followers for the last time at her eighty-sixth birthday celebration. Her final message to them was, "Failure is impossible."

About the Author

Susan Clinton holds a Ph.D. in English and is a part-time teacher of English Literature at Northwestern University in Chicago. Her articles have appeared in such publications as *Consumer's Digest, Family Style Magazine,* and the Chicago *Reader.* In addition, she has contributed biographical and historical articles to *Encyclopaedia Britannica* and *Compton's Encyclopedia,* and has written reader stories and other materials for a number of educational publishers. Ms. Clinton lives in Chicago and is the mother of two boys.

About the Artist

Ralph Canaday has been involved in all aspects of commercial art since graduation from the Art Institute of Chicago in 1959. He is an illustrator, designer, painter, and sculptor whose work has appeared in many national publications, textbooks, and corporate promotional material. Mr. Canaday lives in Hanover Park, Illinois, with his wife Arlene, who is also in publishing.